The Key to Entirety

Grace Miralia

For information contact:
gracekmiralia@gmail.com
Instagram: @gracemiralia
http://www.gracemiralia.com

Book cover design by Cherie Fox
ISBN: 9780999901106

First Edition: June 2020

Dedication...

This book is dedicated to every person who has seen and accepted me for who I am. For everyone who has supported, encouraged, and assisted me on my path of inner healing towards deepest dreams.

To my mother for her flowers,
To my father for his laughs,
To my grandpa for his wisdom,
To my grandma for her nurturing,
To Beth Ann for her love,
To James for his support,
To Anna for everything,
To myself... for the soul searching.
Razi, my love, I couldn't have done this without you.
Marina, I love you endlessly.

Table of Contents

Website: gracemiralia.com
Instagram: @gracemiralia
Twitter: @gracemiralia

Introduction

When I first started writing "The Key to Entirety," I was beginning my inner healing and personal growth journey. I wanted to release old restraints so that I could create a life I truly desired. After a few years of writing, growing, and evolving, the book naturally created itself. I figured these poems could help people in their lives as they did in mine. I figured if I kept them to myself it would be a crime.

My intention is to inspire you towards your dreams while supporting your inner healing journey.

I am so grateful you are choosing to embark on this path with me. May all your dreams and wishes come true in abundance.

With love,
Grace

My Journey to Wholeness

Part One
Healing Myself

Some days it seems I'd rather stay inside and
hide from who I've come to be rather than
simply setting her free.
I do not know how this has come to be,
yet I know I'd like to be free.
And in the process of becoming, how come it
can be so hard to just leap?
So large to reap the benefits of coming home to
me and resting at my own two feet.
I see how far I've come, and I know that I am
young, but is that supposed to free me?
Do you see me past my face, race, or state of
being?
Do you see me past the mask I sometimes show
for, oh, I don't know, days at a time?

I can't hide this fire forever.
She's getting bigger and I don't seek to tame her
anytime soon.
Her name is Tabetha and she will beat my ass if I
don't feed her my dreams.
Because she sees me for who I am,
And that's all I want,
To be seen for who I am.

All that I am makes me all that I'm not.
All that I'm not makes me all that I am.
The breeze, the trees, that is who I am.
Not the superficialities.

I am on my way to find meaning every day
through the lives I touch though some go away.
I am searching for meaning through the light
which casts upon me as I write.

All that I am defines all that I'm not.
Which helps me become all that I want.
All that I am shows me all that I'm not.
And how freeing that can be.

I have used my thoughts to escape reality
before, so this is nothing new for me.
My belief is that by running away from me
I'll somehow become free.
Though this has not come to be, obviously.
I reach out with love, life gives me a tug,
and I run from who I claim to be.
I don't have to be queen,
I just feel that it was made for me.

Where's the sun?
How can I run to her?
What will I say when I arrive at her feet?
I mean look at her, she thrives, and I'm all
alone, don't ask me why.
Some days I'm sane and other days I'm
insane.
Why run from the sun that lives within me?

Some days I cave and other days I crave more
desire from my own soul.
I'd like to think I'm in control but you tell
me.
Maybe that's what it is.
I count on you to tell me what for me but
that's for me to become.
My own sun.
I'd like to.
I'd like to bask in my own rays for days if it'd
save me from this head space.

I'm scared.
I've been there before.
In my mind.
And my mind has not always been kind.
It tries to redefine what is already mine.
What I already see.
What I've already come to be.

I let go.
But for how long?
I don't know.
And it shows.

We do the best we can with the hand we are
dealt and try not to melt under pressure.
I've been told that pressure forms diamonds.
So I guess I am a diamond under a wall of
rocks because I rock my own world.
I've been told I'm in this alone, and if I don't
change, I'll turn to stone.
I have to write it out for it to come about so I'll
say that one day,
when I'm away from this place,
I'll run towards the ocean carrying a thick
heartbeat and a white smile strung across my
face.
My arms spread wide to the sky with sparkles
gleaming in my eyes.
I'll turn around to see all I've become—
Me and me.
You'll see.
You'll see why I've done all this for me.
I started young, at about 19, and that was very
much a woman for me.
I brushed my hair, handled myself with care,
and left home with careful precision.

It's all a process you see,
I've always wanted to be queen,
And someday I'll meet you there.

"I guess all that really matters is that you
grab my hand," I say to my heart.
I express myself through art.
"This is me!" I say to me.
"I can't hide you anymore.
I don't want to deny you anymore.
There is no use in pushing you away."
Breathe into your heart space.
Repeat after me:
"We will always fly, feel me, feel me.
We will always fly, believe me, believe me."

No more hiding this essence.
No more hiding me.
I believe,
I believe,
I believe in me.

I deserve silence.
I deserve sound.
I deserve to turn this all around.
I deserve water.
I deserve air.
I deserve to get the heck out of here.
Just to be led back.
Back to me.
Back to my dreams.
Back to pure belief.
I wash fear out of my hair, strand by strand,
and brush it back just to be safe.
"I've been here before. I've tasted this blood of
defeat."
Of rising past it all, and once again learning how
to stand tall.
Beyond all else.
A well of strength pours its wings over my being.
I've learned to swim and dance in the rain.
To feel what needs to be felt, and sit with it.
"Okay," I say.
"I see. I see clearly. I need not anyone but me.
I need to believe in my own true being."
I see her shine, she is all of me combined.
I touch the clouds and take a bow.

Let's dance it out.
Shake it off.
"Ahhhh!!" I scream.
Whatever.

Let's enjoy this wild ride,
Take this wild advice,
And lie with me beneath the starry sky.
How much is hidden behind the veil of time?
We humans may never truly see all the beauty
that lies within you and me.

Let us rise despite the passing of tides.
Let us beam full of light.

"Get your words out on paper even if it
doesn't make sense," says my mind.
Who seems to be talking all the time.
What will I carry home with me this time,
this experience?
Fall in love with the moment before it slithers
out of your palms.
"You've got this," says my internal
motivational speaker, (whom I appreciate).
Maybe that's why I couldn't crack the code...
"I must let you out!" I silently shout.
And when I envision home, why am I
dancing alone?
"What color is your soul?
What does it look like?" he asked.
"Well, I'm not sure," I say, lying in the bath.
Bubbles bursting.
Tears rolling down my cheeks.
I pat the top of the water like a seal claps his
hands at sea.
"I haven't gotten that far..."
Our eyes meet.
What all creates fate? I wonder.
We can never know unless we try.

If I had a time machine I'd step back to the
first place I carefully set my feet.
Outside in the lovely, full, colorful garden my
mother created just for me.
Almost everything she creates is for me,

(and I don't mean to sound cocky).
What do I miss from my old life and what
memories do I hold onto, tight?
Some things are spoken memories that follow
us to the end of the trail.
"Let it go." I said within my head.
It could be a new leaf.

I don't need sound, I need truth.
I don't need sound, I need truth.
I need to trust more, about what's in store for me.
Yes indeed.
I need to trust more.
I need listeners, I need to listen.
To what comes from within.
Yes that's what it is, I need to listen.
Excuse me if I interrupt but are these words
enough?
Can you hear me,
      me,
           me?
Can you hear me,
      me,
           please?
Why are you pleading now?
What are you looking for that's not stored inside
of you now?
You don't need anyone to understand.
You don't need anyone to grab your hand.
You're true, you're true.
You're you, you're you.
You're alright.
You'll win the fight.
It's alright, it's alright.
Don't cry, don't cry.
Let go now,
just let go.

Let me show you now.
Let me hold you now.
It's time to let go,
now.

Who am I without my family or long list of accomplishments?
Who am I without my singing, dancing, acting, or laughing?
Who am I without my gifts, without the curve of my hips, the soft texture of my lips, or my to do list?

How can I write in a way,
That allows me to look at faith in the eyes,
And still rise high above it?

Something could mean so much to you and you
could only be able to see it once.
To touch it once.
To feel it into being once.
Are you okay with this thought process?
Can you find satisfaction within this knowing?
Around each corner, are you able to find
something that reminds you of home?
Of your holiness?
Your purity?

Let me ask you, how do you do under pressure?
Or when you don't like the weather?
Can you find pleasure within sticky situations?
Can you laugh even when your brain hurts?

States of change, rearranging pace.
Elegant ways throughout the days.

I count on my inner being to lift the fatal flaws
and disguise from my eyes.
We can be anything and that is not
but
a
dream.

This process of healing is not just for me.
It's bigger than that.
It's finding center despite all things around me.
Which surround me, frighten me, and challenge
all I've come to know.
The immersion period.
Submerged in the knowledge of the great
unknown.
Shedding fictional characters I've built
all on my own.
Leading me right back to start, my true state of
heart.
It shows.
Through snow, rain, and pain.
It's under there,
where we sometimes forget to look.
All it took was time to become my own,
and let my past be known.
Let it show, and to this day know that some
days are full of pain.
We strip this away to find its true face which lies
away and tries to define all that we hide deep
inside. For the sake of fear, or whatever else.

As long as there's wind in my sails, I'll grab the
rails, unleash the woman within me.
She leads me home, and though I roam, I know
I've found a place here.

Hold her near,
And in the clear,
I'll dance for you.
I'll tell the truth.

When I wallow is when I truly bloom.
I take hold of all that is true.

I know the power of wisdom.
I know the power of greed.
I know the power of anger.
I know the power of me.

I must own these shadows,
They are mine to keep.
All that I seek,
Lies within them.

In my writing, I am my own friend.
I have my back until the end.
My tears hold years I've spent stuck up
in my own head.
If I can find freedom within my words,
Then it won't matter how much this hurts,
Because I know that there is an end.

There is simple and easy comfort within the
things I know.
That I'm familiar with.
That I've tasted before.
There's comfort in them.
And when I begin releasing all this tension,
I remove my own mask.
I see things for how they really are and realize
there isn't any comfort in the way I used to do
things at all.
In how I push away.

Am I seeking a trace?
For someone to call out my name?
I do seek truth.
No, it's not easy work to do.
Tuning within and feeling unsafe,
there.
But if I had to choose, which I get to every day,
I'd choose me.
I'd choose me surrendering to the lost parts of
me.
Not that I am not already complete,
But that there's still more of me to meet.

Some things are out of control for me.
Meaning if I were to interject them,
I would not get too far.
The only thing that suits my mind,
Is finding time to renew it.

The mind makes up crazy scenarios and swears
that it's right.
We are who we fight for, because it's our right.
So
what if the way I find freedom is within all that
I write?
So
what if I only claim to be who I am tonight?
So
what if my demons win the first fight?
So
what if the sword I choose is a knife?

All that I seed inside me is ingrained.
I feed my own flame.

I am water,
I am rain,
I am dust,
I am pain.

Rise again.
Rise again.

I am water,
I am rain,
I am lust,
I am shame.

Rise again.
Rise again.

The word woman is nothing short of wonder.
From where she came from,
to who she has become.
Past the pain that came into her name.
A world of hurt, she'll rise again.

A woman is a flame.
A woman is a flame.

Watch her burn.
A woman is a flame.

I wish these words could fill,
the spaces between my bones,
and dissolve my fears into nothingness.

I wish,
        I wish,
                I wish.

I can't always be there to fix what is broken.
And sometimes it's true, I lose my focus.
But maybe it's not that way for you.
Maybe you see the truth and know that there's
not much else to lose.
The heart beats again, this is no sin.
Every word I write is a space to live in.

But some things require you to journey deeper.
The path is steeper and you must decide whether
to leap or remain tethered.
I suppose I cannot predict the weather,
whether or not I will leap or remain tethered.
I choose freedom.
Did I really choose life at this time?
Deep emotions are my calling and I realize I
must remain still.
Where's this guidance leading me?
I'd like to go home.
Surround myself in the great unknown.
It is then when I truly understand my power.

And with all tasks at hand, from where I must
end to where I must begin,
I'll rise high when I feel small.
I realize I had created pain from no pain at all.
I won't deny this strength and power within me.
My interests rest at sea,
I soak into the salt and snow,

Create my own pillow.
Close my ears to what I hear,
and listen to what nature knows.
What she knows, without the judgment of my
own ego.
My creativity centers me.
There must not be anything wrong with me.
That is why I must remain true, you see?
This is me.
Basking freely.

I must go.
I must grow.

Without the shadow I would not know how
or where to grow.
I wouldn't know what my soul has to say or
what my true name is.
I wouldn't know what real fame is.
So I come into my own version of all these
things.
I witness castles amongst strong light beings.
I recognize it is within my calling to read into
these things.
For the mark I make will be steamed across my
grave.
And I'll look down from directly above,
With my head resting upon pure desire,
And I'll smile.

To all my friends:
You must know that I will never go on
without you.
All the words I've never said spread
within my head.
I will never leave you, this I know.
And maybe I will always grow away from each
place I get to know.
I answer the calling so I must not be wrong.

I am more than my name.
I am more than my name.
I am more than my name.

How I sit in this space helps me relate to
each state of mind I've ever been.
How I sit and relate determines the state I take
up space within this place.
How I have created my own fate between my
enormous wings that cast a shadow over my
being and keep me safe from unexpected
behavior I thought I had erased.

I love me.

I suppose that's what matters today.

I love me.

I believe in what I create.

I love me.

I'll take that to the grave.
And live on through the shadows of my name.
It is then when I will disperse throughout time
without much thought to it.

Because I believe I will be alright.
Because I believe my soul is right.

Mostly?
Sometimes?
Whatever.
I love me.

Everything I do that's worth doing
influences my growth.
Everything I've created that stands out to me,
I hold close.
I don't always know which way the wind blows,
and I suppose it is not up to me to choose.
But we have choices to make out of moments
which create our lives.
Each day we may die, each day we may rise.
I can't sit here all alone and wonder why.
Freedom casts its spell between my lips
and I'm comfortable with it.
I see the way the day curves into night as
it gleams with wise wisdom of ancient tribes.
Things begin to feel alright when I write.
As if there's no use in feeling as though I have
to choose to fight.

I call in my own antidote; the secret code to all
that goes on within each bone in my body.
I hold space for each character I've grown out of.
Each phase of me that I've let loose.
It's about stripping away each face that no
longer serves me.
Each person has this power.
Each person is a powerful magnet for
every desire.

It's homemade destiny.
There's no use in clinging to the old me.

Cloudless seams, living in a daydream.
Each place I go leads me down a new road.
Wash me away of the days of sorrow that may
remain.
Are there moments when I should run?
I'm sure of who I will become.

The light,
The fight,
The wisdom,
Decisions.

I end here,
which never really ends.
All that must end,
must begin again.

Part Two
Freedom Within

My faith is a tree.
The branches are my wings.
I fly above this place, this city, this earth.
As I look down at all I've left behind,
I blow a kiss, turn my head,
and never look back.
It is then when I soar.

Unveil the mask.
The presence of who I am not,
Uncovers the presence of who I eternally am.
I release all attachments.
Everything I feel is beautiful.
All that I see right now, is right.
It all has a placement within something bigger
than me.
I am happy to be a part of this puzzle,
this game.
To rest on a throne of peace that came from
within me.

I've done this all before.
I've suffered the paradox.
Just to be sweetly reminded of all that truly is
and ever will be.

When I connect to my heart,
I know where to start.
As I complete myself,
As I complete my being,
Starting clean, beginning over and over again,
There's only one heart song.
Which beats alongside tribal drums.
And as time goes on, it's just me and my heart
song.
So I sing along, long, long,
to my heart song, song, song.
"We are all one, one, one,
under the sun, sun, sun.
Growing, flowing, all at once."

If I want it, I grab it.
It can be so simple you see.
What you let in is what you choose to set free.
To free the soul is to take control.
I take hold of the being who lives within me.
I grab her hands as she expands.
I resonate with her,
She is my friend until the end.

I am grateful for those loving hands who grasp
me.

Learning how to be there for myself is the
greatest gift I could give to myself.
It doesn't have to be forced.
It's just me being me, choosing to be free, and
owning who I am as a divine human being.
It's about celebration, initiation into what rings
true for me.

But sometimes we lose our footing.
We get caught up in who knows what with who
knows who.
But we must not confuse what rings true for us
and what matters to whom.
In other words, we must trust ourselves above all
else.
Because each of us is a divine flower with petals
all our own.
All within various shapes and sizes of evolution.
We have the power to choose for us.
The rest is simply nuts.

I carry words of favor on my shoulders.
You cannot take this strength away from me.
I protect what is mine this time.
You cannot take this strength away from me.

I've moved away from the face I once was.
From the place that swept me off my feet and
laid me down with the devil.
My man made, heart saved devil.
And it was all make believe you see.
I was caught up in a whirlpool of thought,
Searching for a way to live out my name.
There is no way, only today, and choices to make.
This is the best way to play.

I own my inner fire.

As long as I love me I don't need anyone else to
see me for who I am.
I hold and grasp the way that I am, firmly, and
there's no need for anything about it to change.
Unknowingly, I changed, and evolved,
once I decided to take a step back and release
it all.
Expectation, angst, worry,
I let go of it all.
That in itself helps me stand tall.
I don't expect much of anything yet I must be
happy.
Make it happen for me and the person I am
becoming.
Words on the paper, these words on the paper,
they connect me to something much bigger than
me.
I believe in these words on this paper.

I write down feelings until my brain hurts,
Thoughts disperse,
Silence prevails,
A deep inhale.
Release.
My brain washes down to my feet.
Release.
I've made it home now.
I feel alone somehow but this space cradles my
being.
She knows how to take care of me.

I relax so that I'll later know how to make the
plunge towards the sun.
The fun of it all, the risk of the fall.
Each step I've decided to take has carved out a
shape.
It's a straight shot, or so I thought, but now I see
that it's wavy.
The opportunity to see the world all on my own.
The opportunity to know myself as I've never
known.

I can rest knowing that I do my best.
I can rest knowing that there is no test.
Only light, only dark.

I am not scared.
For I know that I will be there.

The fruit of my effort lies within my truth.
I stand firm.
I take root into the future.
Into all that I'll ever seek to be.

I woke up dancing.

Yes, it's true. I really woke up dancing.
There I was in a new place, laying down in bed,
submerged in covers of various quilts and fluffy
pillows.

I woke up dancing.

As I opened my eyes,
I peeked around the room.
Silence—for a moment.
Then birds made their way in and began
singing a tune.
The same tune they always do.

I woke up dancing.

I jumped to the edge of the bed, my legs hanging
off the ledge, I opened my arms wide to the sky
and hugged the open space before me.

I rise.

Tiptoeing from the bed, down the hall, and
into the living room where I was greeted by the
morning sun.

A luxurious space.

I woke up dancing.

Then I noticed my legs felt tight.
"Why? Oh yeah!" I thought.
I walked far and wide yesterday night.
It must be time to shake it off.
One foot, two foot, shake your toosh!

I woke up dancing.

The world is quite a mysterious place,
wouldn't you say?
We never know what to expect or what we are
gonna get next.
But I don't fear it.
For I know that I will always wake up dancing.

Take me away,
With the sun rays.
My scattered brain,
Finally falls away.
Take me away.
Take me away.
Let me see the way.

Lay me down,
With your soft sound.
Feel the waves,
Rest upon my name.

My scattered brain,
Seeks a way,
To bloom and grow.
Let go of what I know.
Let go of what I know.

Lay me away,
In sacred space.
So that I may pray,
For one more day.

You may not see,
You may not be,
All that you know,
All that you seek.
Yet I believe,
In order to be free,
We must believe,
In what we don't see.

Part Three
Angels Inside

Who I am is who I am.
Who I am is a trillion atoms and a dozen
shapes.
Who I am is a bundle of joy, abundant, and
safe.
Despite the waves of motion,
Keeping me grounded,
Giving me space.

Who I am is a starseed, blessed by the Gods.
Who I am is fragile, darkness, shadow.
Who I am is changing, rearranging, taking
shape.
Forcing movement beneath my name.

My Grace,
My strength,
It does not end here within this physical body.
Who I am changes and molds by the day.
It molds as I play.

I am not ashamed of this flame.
Birthed inside this cave of mine, oh so divine.
You could try to stomp it out,
Water it down,
But you just might find this well of mine,
oh so divine, cannot be led astray.
I will be here until the earth won't turn and the
stars don't burn.
I'll be here changing, rearranging, taking shape.
Until I am rebirthed as a Goddess who rests at
sea.
And even then you see, I'll still be forming
wings.
Because this inner being of mine is ever
beaming.
Full of light.

I grew up with curls in my hair that ran along
beside me as I trotted across my mother's garden.
It always made me feel more free as I learned
how to become me.
The essence of flow, floating past the evergreens.
I forever dream of bright white clouds dipping
down into blue ocean waters.
I rest my head well at night knowing I'll spend
eternity there.
But until then, I'll spend my days here, being
divine.
For it is my natural birthright.

You are not your mind.
You are not your mind.
        You are you.
You are you.
        Free to flow,
Free to go home.
Where you may know,
Now,
        now,
                now.
I love you,
Now,
        now,
                now.
I seek you,
Out,
        out,
                out.
I breathe you,
Out,
        out,
                out.
Ahhh...
        Ahhh...
                Ahhh...
Feel me singing,
My ears are ringing.
I hear you kiss the sun,
I run, run, run!

I will meet you on the other side of here.
And forever more,
I rise.
Like the tides.
And wish upon the stars,
They leave sparkles in my eyes.
They align.
I unwind.
I ride the wave,
       I kiss your face.
           I soar.
Above this place.
       Beyond the gates.
           White picket fence.
I bless the end of time.
I bless the end of time.
Stars,
      mars,
           me.
A queen of queens.
Rest upon my throne.
I'm coming home.
      I rise.
I cannot deny the truth.
      I rise.
I blame you, shadow flame.
I blame you.
      Rest now.
Upon the clouds.
      Rest now.

I believe you now.
Rest.
  Sound.
    Sleep.
      Gone.
        Me.

Rose gold butterflies.
Rose gold, time flies.
One day I may die,
The next day I may rise.
Rose gold butterflies.

Your Path

Part One
Inner Healing

Healing is a process that anyone can take.
And sometimes it does not feel great.
It's the risks that we take,
The moments we create,
The hearts we heal,
The time it seals our fate.
Everyday is a new way to change.
To grow,
To fall,
To feel small.
None of it is wrong, all of it is normal, and
all of it has a place here.
You'll always have a place here,
even when you feel small.

And on days when you feel tall,
Show the world all that you are.
How beautiful, smart, and loving you are.
Because we need you.
We need you here.
It's okay to feel small.
It's okay to feel small.
Because feeling small is not really being small
at all.

If you think about it, no one's felt the way you
have felt, not exactly.
Not with your experiences, thoughts, emotions,
and perspectives.
No, no one knows your mind.
Therefore no one can tell you what is real,
How to feel,
Or that you're wrong.
You are you, they are they.
And that is more than okay.

Some things don't need to be explained.
They just need to be felt, embraced,
and then let go.

Sit on it. Just sit on it.
There's no need for a direct answer on
anything, (except when it's rent day).
In order to reach a new place of growth,
We must find our wings amongst chaos,
Dust ourselves off after a windstorm,
And find safe spaces within new grounds, new
territory, new and fertile soil.
It's necessary to count all the things you're
doing *right.*
Take care of yourself as you would a newborn
child.
And remember to be kind to your mind because
you've never been in this stage of evolution
before.
Evolution, resolution, revolution...
We're all here together.

You're never too old to try.
It's okay to cry.
These setbacks are not meant for you to lose.
You've got what it takes to choose the life that's
right for you.

The divine process of life.
We are pulled through struggles
and difficult times only to find wisdom
waiting for us on the other side.

Do not fear growth.
It comes in all ways, shapes, and forms,
and pain is the most common.

We must be ready to let go of all that does not
serve us in order to become who we really are.
I've learned that emotions must be felt to be
released, and it may feel uncomfortable.
But anytime you feel discomfort, anytime you
cry, say to yourself,
"Thank goodness this is happening!
I am releasing!
I am letting go!
I am moving on."
Sometimes you don't need to know why.
So just keep moving forward.
Do not stop.
It will be worth it because it makes you stronger.

Do not hide from who you are.
Let your desires show their face.
Let your shadows come out to play.
Do not hide from who you are.
Listen to yourself.

You don't have to fit in, stand out, stand out!
You don't have to be thin, you don't have to be
stout.
You don't have to understand everything or
anything right now.

Transmute your fire into pure desire.
Turn disgrace into faith.
Turn hope into knowing.
And dance until all else fades away.

Let your heaviness smile up at you and say,
"Hey, I know you'll be okay.
Hey, watch the way you talk to yourself today.
You're okay.
You're okay.
You're okay.
Your face *is* the way it's supposed to be shaped.
Your weight *is* the way it's supposed to weigh.
Your freckles, your dimples, your curves…
You are the way you are supposed to be today."

No, there's nothing wrong with you.
Put your bags down.
Dance around.
Act a clown.
You are safe and sound.
On the ground.
Here and now.
You are safe and sound.

Part Two
The Path of Purpose

Who are you to you,
When you're all alone in your room?
Listen to your soul,
What is it telling you to do?

The only thing that will ever truly make us happy
is going for what we want.
Going for what our soul wants.
The path of purpose.
No pile of money, relationship, house, vacation,
or material object will ever satisfy the space we
have carved out in our hearts to reach our
highest potential.
Living here on earth and making space for our
passions is our right.
It is our job and lifetime journey to reach within
ourselves and find a well of strength.
Strength that gives us the will to continue and
take shape.
Strength that gives us the ability to continue
on our very own special paths, no matter what
shows up in our spheres.
No matter what the world tells us to show up for
or as.

We will continue to grow and prosper when we
live within the truth.
When we dedicate our minds to evolution.
Personal, beautiful evolution.
Nothing else will suffice.

It is of great value to know the difference
between what the head wants
and what the heart wants.
What the soul wants.
Not what we're told to want, not what we no
longer resonate with, but what we continually
have faith in.
Where we find our place in.
What lies beneath the skin.
What hides from the sunlight and thrives in the
night sky.
Where our mind ends, our heart begins.
Where our heart begins, there is a space worth
spending time in.

Sometimes we cannot make use of all the thoughts that swirl around in our minds, so why try?

We can only do so much when it comes to change—making a change, being the change, setting ourselves up for an upgrade.

So more than anything, we must set ourselves up for patience and trust that perfect timing is on the way.

We must avoid the things that leave us uninspired or drain our spirits.

We deserve to feel good, do good, and be good. For ourselves and others.

Some things take longer than others.
Within each process there is truth, there is
harmony, there is wisdom.
Walking by faith does not entail walking blindly
into all that we love or seek.
It means walking with Grace, strength, and
knowing we will be okay.
There are so many reasons as to why we must try.
As when we try, we grow.
Despite the circumstances or outcomes.

There's wisdom in waiting.
In patience,
Debating,
What you are creating.
In order to uncover your symptoms of greatness,
There's wisdom in waiting.

Breathe in, breathe out.
Watch your dreams come about.
Breathe in, breathe out.
You're on the way.
You're on the way home.
And it'll be better than you've ever known.

Take your time, you will learn how to steer in the
driver's seat of your life.
Keep in mind all the places you've come from
and how fast you've arrived.
Have patience with all your desires and you will
thrive.

Take care of your goals and visions.
Especially the body you live in.
Even if you have to work a job you hate to get the
bills paid, keep your dreams within your mind's
eye so that you do not forget them.
You're here on earth with visions for a reason.
So that you can live to develop and experience
them.
Don't forget to live them.
Don't forget to live.

Never lose sight of who you are at heart.
Don't let others push you away from your soul.
Put yourself first.
There are always going to be distractions.
Remember to stay focused in your direction—
moving forward.
Be mindful of who you surround yourself with.
You've got what it takes to be successful.
You don't need to be anything but yourself.

In order to truly be happy, we must embrace every part of ourselves.
All of ourselves.
Mistakes, phases of being, and dreams of becoming.
In order to break free from who we have been we must push past the fear of becoming who we dream to be.
The self we're often told we do not have what it takes to become.
But guess what?
We do have what it takes.
We must believe in our hearts, souls, and true beings.
It takes great courage,
Yet it is the only way to be free.
Do you want to be free?
Guess what?
You already are, love.
Pay no mind to the haters, disbelievers, especially those who stem from your own mind.

This is your life, love.
Go forth and show them.
Go forth and live.
Leap.

Part Three
Love Yourself

We are human.
The sooner we accept it's normal to be
imperfect,
The sooner we can learn to love ourselves.
Loving ourselves is not something we are
usually taught.
It is a journey we must consciously
choose to embark upon.
Once we learn to love ourselves, we can
extend that love outwards into the world.
But we cannot give from an empty cup.

It all starts with the self.
Putting ourselves first is the ticket to
freedom.
It creates stability within all aspects of our
lives: relationships, work, play, and leisure.
It provides us the means to show up as our
best selves within all situations.
We must give to ourselves without
reservation.
It is then when we truly fly.

The gift of giving.
First to self, then to others.
Love—
The gift that keeps on giving.
Despite all temporary circumstances.
One of the only aspects of life that is eternal is love.
It must be fostered towards the self and then it can be extended outwards.
We will never be able to give to others if we do not first give to ourselves.

Just like any love, self-love needs to be cultivated,
over time, naturally.
There is no need to rush it.
There's no need to fuss over the process.
It is an opportunity to grow and blossom.

Just like any love, self-love has value.
It means something to me,
It means something to you.

We must not only be there and show
ourselves love when times are easy.
We must stick around for ourselves during
difficult times as well.
It is then when we must cherish our bodies.
It can be easier to deny ourselves—to turn the
other cheek, especially when we are in need.
Yet, the only way to grow and evolve is to
embrace contrasting emotions and experiences
so that we can see things for how they really are.

There is no use in denying the truth.
There is no use in denying you.

We may not always take into acount the
things that are truly not good for us.
The situations and people who are not
good for us.
We may love them,
We may want to protect them,
When what we really must do is protect
ourselves.

You don't have to play these roles anymore.
Of taking care of everyone,
Feeding into negative relationship patterns,
You can choose right now, in this moment,
to change.
It's all a choice.
Everything is a choice.

We must be all that we can be for ourselves, not
deny it.
Each day we try our best, each day we pass our
test.
There is no right or wrong, simply choices.
Choices that may not always be so simple.
The more we give to ourselves, the more we can
give to others.
In the form of love, understanding, honor, and
hope.
We may never be perfect.
We may never have all the answers to our
questions.
But we do have time.
We do have now.
And it is up to us to make use of it in all the ways
we can.

Trust yourself.
Be the light.
Listen.
Why go against yourself?
Why follow through with something that will not
serve you long term?
Treat yourself right.
Love where you are.
Embody your truth.
All of you.
Every face, state, all of you.
Who you may be afraid to show,

Where you may never let yourself go.
You have power and light to share.
You must not be ashamed of the color of your
hair.
You are beauty, power, and strength.
You know, you understand what's at stake.
The more you let go, the more you let it flow.
So let go to let it flow.
As you understand yourself, you understand the
masses.
How others may think,
How others may feel.

Part Four
Unboundedness

When we embody our truth,
We become one with it,
And all we ever need follows thereafter.
We must have the courage to embark on our
personal journeys and grow within our hearts.
We must trust that what we need will come when
we need it, with belief in ourselves, our ideas,
and the Universe.
It all starts with us.

Freedom of life is purely in the hands of those
who create it.
Molding various shapes and sizes of reality.
Shades of grey, rays of sunshine alike.
I believe that freedom lies within the individual.
Each star from the night sky showing us ways to
go and ways to grow.
The path—never ending, and why would we
want it to?
Where are we running to?
What are we running from?
Each of us is a unique expression of nature.
Our own minds are our own kinds of beauty.

We have the ability to shift our perceptions and morph into who we want to be. (Maybe not a cat, but you know).

We can create what we want in our lives.

How we grew up doesn't have to define *who* we decide to be, or *who* we end up as.

If we want to be different, all we have to do is decide to be different, and act accordingly.

We must not worry about the things we cannot change.
We must focus on the thoughts, actions, and habits we can change now and in all of time that follows.
We must learn how to improve our lives and know that it always starts and ends with us.
All that we need is inside of us.
We must learn to grow and prosper in the ways that matter to us.

Silence brings clarity, while clarity brings sound,
which turns all things around.
Where you want to go you're free to roam.
There are no limits to your growth.
Breathe in, breathe out.
Watch your dreams come about.
The clarity you seek is within your bones.
It goes down to your toes.
You are not weak if you have yet to know where
you want to go.
For you will be shown.
Know that you have grown.
This is the process of life and it doesn't
happen overnight.
It's not supposed to.
Rejoice in the choice.
You get what you give and receive what you
believe.
You're an infinite flower ready to bloom.
Discover all the room you can create when you
clear out self hate.
There's no single way to choose a life that's
meant for you.
It's all up to you.
Being able to step into your power, really
honing it is when true healing begins.
Because it's where your life begins.

Everyday is an opportunity to grow and
experience new things.
Every time we take a moment to reflect upon
our hearts desires, it brings us closer to our
soul's purpose, our true essence, and our inner
truth.
Everyday is an opportunity to unite with who
we are and learn about the Universe.
We have endless opportunities in life, what it
has to offer us, and what we in turn can offer
the world.
So much can be accomplished for everyone.

Some things don't need to be defined and all
things come with time.
We must accept things as they evolve.
Not everything is beautiful, yet it is all beautiful.
What's inside can be transformed and what's
outside is where dreams are formed.

As we seek truth in what is "unknown" we start
to realize what is "true" is not really true at all.
It's the secrets behind the walls.
We come to see all we can be.
The essence of becoming.
You can be who you want to be.
There's nothing false about this theory.

Learn what you need to learn, grow how you
need to grow, and go where you need to go.
Nothing can hold you back from this show,
Besides your ego.
Follow your own truth.
It can only come from you.
It can only come about if you choose.
In this moment.
Here and now.
It's all within the process of becoming.

Whether we consciously or unconsciously
acknowledge it, Spirit is always there for us.
We are never alone in any of our endeavors and
everything is set up for us divinely.
We have decisions to make as to what we want
to create in our lives, but we are each given a
blueprint to follow.
We find it within our hearts.
Anything that shows up on our path is by no
means an accident.
Everything serves a purpose.

It's not about other people, it's about you.
It's about your growth and what you know to be
true.
Cultivate a life of your dreams.
Let all you'd like to see come to be.
Believing in yourself has nothing to do with
anyone else.
You know who you are.
That's what matters here.

Forget the ideas that others embed in your head.
You know what you're about.
And so what if it doesn't come out exactly the
way you thought it would.
Life is made for exploring, experiencing different
phases of being, and of becoming.
Life is about meeting the unknown,
And getting to know it.
All that is unknown will show as we grow.
It is never as serious as it seems to be.
So go ahead,
We are all free.

It's not a hindrance if you do not
allow it to be.
Any excuse as to why you won't rise,
Is an illusion that can be transcended.

Remember to be yourself,
Remember to free yourself.

Soak in the moment, really own it.
Focus on where you are.
You've never been here, at this place and time
before.
You're stronger than you were before.
Soak in the moment, really own it.
Integrate your experiences and cultivate
your expressions.
Live true, live for you.
Because it's all for you to choose.

What really matters is what's in our hearts,
How we express our truth to the world,
And what we spend our time doing.

Each day is an expansion of what we once knew,
An extension of who we are becoming,
And how we live out our truth.
This holds great value.

As we cultivate our greatest gifts and share them
with the world,
We give ourselves and others permission to live in
truth and harmony.
We are each given unique abilities and messages
to express.
And if we keep them to ourselves,
We can become depressed.

We must not hide anymore.
We must walk with faith and determination
towards the things that call out our names.
We must believe in ourselves and our brothers
and sisters of the earth, for we are all here
together.
We may live separate lives but that does not mean
we are truly separate.
Everything we do affects each other, like a ripple
effect.
We must act as a team.
Fully embracing each other in the process of
healing, becoming, and evolution.

It is a shame that society today is so separated.
It is celebrated to be alone.
Don't get me wrong, personalized achievements
are great and should be accounted for.
Yet during times of trials and tribulations across
the globe is when we need each other most.

We all want to be happy.
We all want to be free.
Do we seek peace and serenity?
What do we want our earth to look like?
Take a moment.
We must learn to put our differences aside in
order to reach a higher, greater good.

End Note

I want to end by saying, remember to be patient with yourself on your inner healing and personal growth journey. We are continuously growing, evolving, and realizing more truth about ourselves.

No one can tell you who or what you are, and the answers you seek are within your heart.

You already are all that you seek, and that is The Key to Entirety.

Made in the USA
Coppell, TX
02 September 2020